The Doors Swing Both Ways

By: Deon Harris

Copyright © 2017 Deon Harris

All rights reserved.

First print 2017 June

This is a book of fiction. Any references or similarities to actual events, real people, or real locations are intended to give the novel a sense of reality. Any similarity to other names, characters, places and incidents are entirely coincidental.

All right reserved. No part of this book may be reproduced in any form, or by any means without prior consent of the author and publisher as a collective, except brief quotes used in reviews.

ISBN-13:978-1695714304

Cover Design: Crystell Publications

Book Productions: Crystell Publications
You're The Publisher, We're Your Legs
We Help You Self Publish Your Book
(405) 414-3991
www.crystellpublications

The Basic Essentials of Doing Time Constructively

DEDICATION

This book is dedicated to the people who are going through some difficulties. I want to tell you and SHOW you that's there's ease after difficulties, there's calm after every storm. To the naysayers that say we can't change or progress after prison - with the grace and mercy from God, anything's possible. The Lord works in mysterious ways and never makes mistakes. By reading this, you're showing that you're ready to refocus and rechannel for the better. Let's do this together.

CONTENTS

	Acknowledgments	vi
1	The Beginning	1
2	Process for the Progress	4
3	Freedom Ride	7
4	Halfway is the Best Way	16
5	This Game Is Economic	27
6	Self-Advocacy	31
7	Faith - On God's Time	33
8	The Formula	35
9	Grinding All My Life	38
10	Delegated Authority	41
11	Obey or Pay	44
12	Another Victory	46
13	Figure It Out	49
14	Passion Came From Pain	52
15	Simply Beautiful	55

Deon Harris

ACKNOWLEDGMENTS

Once again, the part where I spotlight those I love and to whom I owe a profound debt of gratitude. First of all, I give all the honors, praises and endless worship to my personal Lord and Savior Jesus Christ, for not only giving me the mental ability to write and share another story, but most of all for having His grace, mercy and protection that allowed me to make it through, all in one piece. And to everyone on Earth that made my reentry a wondrous and joyous transition, it was greatly appreciated.

Thank you to my darling parents, Mr. & Mrs. Charles and Sandra Boss. Thanks to my other family members and friends. Thanks to the Federal Bureau of Prisons. Thanks to the companies that employed me and helped me get established - Precision Drywall, Whirlpool, Dupaco, Pat McGrath and West Rock.

Thanks to everyone in the old neighborhood who helped me distribute my book and do a makeover to my street image. Shout out to Candace and Tasha at the Beauty Shop. Thanks to my main man Pooh from Unique Beauty Products. Pooh has always been supportive. He gives good, genuine advice on all sorts of topics pertaining to a positive life. He's wants to see me win. He's sold books for me and every time he tells someone to support his main man, that's what those people do. Big thanks to Big Homey, owner of Unique Beauty Products (even though he's younger than me).

Thanks to Austin and his whole family, especially his sister Shaniece, who's the reason for me meeting Pastor Dawson. Thanks to Al and all the barbers at Stay Sharp Barber Shop. Al and I have always had good chemistry and a strong friendship. He let me interact with and sell to his customers, and I appreciated that. Boost Mobile is actually where I got my first cell phone upon reentry into the free world. They also let me interact with their customers. They let me leave fliers and business cards with their customers. Thanks to the workers at the Sinclair station, Jodi and Ann, who helped me when I was starting to distribute my books. That belief in me was appreciated.

My Precision Drywall family (first job post-reentry) really stepped up and helped me get on my feet. I will always cherish my experience with all of them; Dave, Ms. Reel, Ms. Stephens, Eric, Rodney, Jeff, and the other countless workers that all helped me. Two people, Ms. Stephens and Ms. Reel, even let me use their personal cars to practice driving with me so I could be prepared to test for my license. And I can't forget my two main guys, Rio and Sixteen, who helped me get the job. Justin at ESP3 (next door to Precision Drywall) helped me create t-shirts with my logo on them to help create and position my brand.

And finally, my thanks to the whole Hinzman Center staff. My apologies in advance if I forget to list someone. Thank you to Mr. Sam Black, Mr. Booty Gabe, Ms. Donna, The Lovely Ms. Tasha (no longer there), Ms. Julie, Ms. Linda, Ms. Denise (no longer there), Ms. Chris, Courtney, Rashad, Mr. Harris (no longer there), the midnight staff Ms. Gertrude Peterson and Ms. Jamie, Scott, Chad, Pat and everyone else, even the staff ladies who prepared meals. And very special thanks to my supervised release officer.

And to all whom I forgot to mention, you're the best.

Deon Harris

Chapter 1

The Beginning

I want to start by giving all the glory to God for allowing these words to not only be spoken but written from here in the free world. A lot has changed for the good and for the bad since that last time I've been in the free world. Allow me to introduce myself to you. My name is Deon Harris. Mr. Deon Terrell Harris, if you want to get technical or want the correct name on the check. I've been home, or reunited back into society, for 2 ½ years from doing 16 years in federal prison. My original sentence was 360 months. Now by no means am I speaking on it like it's a badge of honor because truthfully speaking, I lost a lot to prison, not just time. But I gained so much wisdom and life during those years away from my freedom! I'm here now, praise God. What I realized in all my years being incarcerated is that God is the most important thing. Your health and freedom are the next two most important things. Let me restate that. God, first and foremost. Health and freedom after that.

I'm going to give you all a journey through my life from the very moment I stepped out into society on free soil, to my encounter in the Gerald R. Hinzman Center (aka the halfway house), my first job, the feeling of reuniting with my mother, father, daughter and family. I get teary-eyed just thinking about that day. Seeing my old friends. Just having to stay focused. I always say and know that I'm one bad decision from being right back in that jail cell and having to go through the pain and hurt all over again. But know this: I cannot and will not put myself through that. I will not put my darling mother, Mrs. Sandra Boss, through that. I won't put any of my family through that.

I know that I have choices. And I explored my options by the grace of God while I was incarcerated. I let the time work for me because I saw those days ahead while I was doing a 360-month sentence. My point is: Never, I mean NEVER, lose faith and hope, no matter what circumstances life puts you in. Trouble doesn't last and time shall pass - I can attest to it.

I've met some very positive people out here in the land of the free, the land of freedom. From various jobs I've worked, my supervised release officer, and all other kinds of post-incarceration relationships. See I'm not confused. I put myself in that bad predicament, but I also got myself out of that bad predicament. I'm always ready. I'm doing nothing illegal. I'm always sober, positive and productive. Living life like my company motto says: Progress Platform.

What can I say other than the man up above has really been blessing me with so much, starting with just being able to come and go as I please. What the average person takes for granted such as being able to go to his refrigerator, using the restroom in peace, or just sitting on the couch watching TV. But most important, to me, is the ability to sit in silence. To just sit still, to BE still. Silence is a true gift. Silence was taken from me once upon a time, and I'll never forget the pain of that. It's not hard for me to be by myself, with no one but God, because I've always felt God's presence. He's given me these words to speak as I write. There's so much color out here.

Now by no means am I saying I'm a saint. Far from it. But the temptation of jeopardizing my freedom is not even in my blueprint. There's rules and regulations out here, and I play by them because I want and will stay in the life of freedom. There's a lot of brothers and sisters that's still in the system. They keep me grounded. I still converse with a lot of brothers on the inside with letters, pictures, money, encouragement. But most of all, my brothers are in my prayers. They just keep me humble. I have nothing to prove to anyone but God. They say when you get older, you obtain some wisdom. Here's some wisdom from me: Prison will either make you better. Or it will make you worse.

CHAPTER 2

The Process For Progress

I can tell you it's easy being locked up. NO responsibility with bills, temptations or the struggles of the everyday world. But being away from my freedom for so long made me kinda scared to face my upcoming freedom. I knew when I got out, I was going to become a productive member of society. And I had prepared myself through the years so whenever the opportunity presented itself, I was not only going to be ready but I was going to bring my best self to the surface. Tupac said, "Penitentiary is packed with promise makers." I was one of those promise makers. I made a vow and a promise to God and myself. God first and then myself. Without God I was nothing. I promised that I was going to bring my best self into freedom.

It was March 14, 2017 when I got a call from the office. The officer on the other end of the phone said, "Can we have inmate Harris 08746-029 to RD please?" The officer called me and I was already prepared, ready to face one of my toughest challenges in life; freedom. I grabbed my gym bag with a couple of possessions in it. All I had that mattered to me was some pictures and a couple of personal items I'd be taking to the halfway house. All the other property I had accumulated over the years I had mailed to my mom's house. So, the officer called for me. I said my goodbyes to a couple of guys, hugged my main man Edward Parker, and stepped out of that housing unit. March 14, 2017 was a snowy day. I had butterflies, and all kinds of thoughts were going through my mind as I walked to the RD. Every guy I passed at the compound knew exactly where I was headed, from the bright new grey jogging suit & new gym shoes, to the fresh haircut and the pep in my step. Yes, it was snowing outside, but the air was starting to feel and smell different with every step of the way. On my walk to the RD I didn't look back. I didn't talk to anyone. I was about the face the world, and that was a lot to take in.

Once I made it to the RD, I could hardly wait to hear the sound of the voice saying the thing I'd been yearning to hear for 16 years. The voice that said, "Harris, you going home". When I heard that I couldn't help but smile from ear to ear, showing all my teeth. When I got there, they made me sit in the very same bullpen I sat in when I came to this prison, 14 months ago after leaving Pekin. Even if they were trying to inconvenience me by having me wait in that bullpen, it was alright by me. One thing I've learned in all my time behind bars is patience. And I'm not confused about the process of leaving prison. It's easy to get here, but very hard to leave. They have to make sure they're letting the right inmate out. So there's fingerprints, paperwork and buttons to be pressed for a person's release. Patience. As I sat in the bullpen for the last time, I thought about how it was a long time coming. And by the grace and mercy from God I MADE IT.

As my thoughts were racing through my mind and I was taking in the sights and smells of the holding area, I heard the sound of the cold click from the keys opening the door. "Harris!" I was about to take my last walk through jail/hell. I've learned so much about myself and about the life I wanted for myself. As I walked to the cashier's window, they asked my name and inmate number for the last time.

They handed me the following:
    A Greyhound bus ticket and my bus route number
    $200 in cash
    A debit card that held the rest of my personal money
    My birth certificate and social security card
    My prison ID

That was it. Nothing more, nothing less. No Rolex watch for retirement. No balloons, no Hallmark card. Just those things listed above and a cab waiting outside to take me to the bus station. I was on my way to be reunited back into society.

CHAPTER 3

Freedom Ride

Close your eyes and just picture this for a second. You've been living in an area that is no bigger than a washroom in a Chicago Housing Authority (CHA) housing project. You've been SHARING that space with someone else, 24/7. A small, tight space, shared with another person. Now open your eyes. You're about to be released from that literal prison, that confinement, that restricted life. Your world is about to explode with freedom, space, options.

As I walked out the last door of the prison TO MY FREEDOM from incarceration, words could not possibly express my joy. I've never won an NBA game. Never won a Superbowl championship. But I was about to get the greatest prize of all - my freedom. Remember, it was a cold, gloomy March day. But the weather didn't matter. All I could hear was The Temptations singing, "I got sunshine on a cloudy day." It was like finally getting a drink after walking in the desert for days. It was like the rainbow after the storm. I can only paint this picture for people who have known the feeling of doing time. It's a beautiful, refreshing thing. It's amazing and powerful. I still get teary-eyed thinking about how my life was on PAUSE for 16 years. By no means do I wish that anyone else SHOULD know that feeling. But if you've done the time, you will definitely want to feel this feeling. The feeling of FREEDOM. As the fresh air hit me, all I could say was, "Thank you, Jesus". There MUST be a God. I MADE IT.

Outside the prison there was a cab waiting to take me to the bus station. I got into the cab, sat there for a minute and just exhaled. I could finally breathe again. I had gotten out of prison the right way, by the grace of God. I keep giving Him the praises cause if there WASN'T a God, you wouldn't be getting this version of this book. Guaranteed.

The cab driver was a male Caucasian who appear to be in his early 50's, heavy-set, short, greyish hair - he looked a little like Alfred Hitchcock. He was very mild-mannered, friendly and was quick to engage in a conversation with me. We were in a conversation, but my mind was racing. I kept thinking about my mother, father and daughter. I WAS ABOUT TO HUG THEM! I was also thinking about some of the brothers I grew to love that I was leaving behind.

We drove and talked, drove and talked. The driver shared some current events with me. He brought me up to speed on Trump, and shared his point of view about Trump being our president and commander in chief. At that point, Trump had only been in office 3 months, and so much was going on in the world. I don't really get into politics, but I was thinking I had gotten out at a good time, coming out to a whole different world. I missed both terms of former President Barack Obama. But thank God for Obama. In fact, Obama reduced my last sentence.

My freedom ride in that cab was amazing. I was all ears, absorbing and receiving all the information and conversation the cab driver wanted to share with me. I kept taking in my surroundings. I was amazed by all the different European car shops. I was amazed by the traffic - it was like being in Disney World in Orlando, Florida. The cab driver shared that he was retired, so I imagined that he had taken numerous people on this same type of ride. Even though he may have taken many on this same ride, I knew I was the one that was NOT going to return to prison, and would NOT ever be going on this ride again. I'm pretty sure I had a look of determination in my eyes, and I hoped the cab driver could sense my humility. This experience was important. So important that I NEVER wanted to do it again. The cab driver dropped me off at the bus station in Youngstown, Ohio. My reentry was in full swing.

Step 1 - Boarding the Bus - Youngstown, Ohio

While I was still incarcerated, I was used to being watched and monitored by officers. Even so, I displayed integrity. I knew I had to be all-in when the time came for me to reenter society. I knew when I got out, I couldn't just wander around, looking for alcohol, drugs or girls. No. I needed to step into the future with purpose. So I started thinking that way before I even got free. Being mentally prepared didn't make it any easier to enter the bus station in Youngstown, Ohio. It was funny because I knew that I had to watch myself. I knew I had to do the right thing. RIGHT NOW. Entering the bus station really represented entering the journey of the rest of my life.

The ghetto feel of the bus station hadn't changed. Drugs and alcohol were still winning. The pains and struggles of everyday life were weighing heavy on some people. You see, one of the good things in prison is that everyone is persevering, getting rest, eating three times a day. People are pretty clean for the most part, with good access to showers. In the free world, right in front of me at the bus station, that was not the case. So my antenna were up, I was on alert and using my survival instincts.

Remember, I was wearing my jail jogging suit and I had the glow of freedom around me. It was obvious that I was different, that I wasn't from "around here". I was "fresh meat", as we say in prison. By no means do I practice looking hard or tough, but I knew I was being sized up by people in the bus station. At that time, I decided I needed to have that "don't mess with me" look in my eyes. I sat there with that look for about six hours. I just observed. And I thought to myself, I'm finally here, back in the real world, the Apollo of Life. And like my brother Rail says, "You ain't about to get booed back off this stage!" I think I got up to use the restroom twice. The bus terminal worker offered me some donuts that were about an hour old, but I was used to that. In prison, we were eating food that was outdated for years, so an hour was nothing. My bus was scheduled to leave Youngstown at 11:00 PM.

Step 2 - En Route - Cleveland, Ohio

The next stretch of the journey felt like a small piece of Heaven and it brought more revelations. I was used to being in shackles from head to toe and with an officer holding a shotgun, just in case. On the bus, none of that. In prison, the officers are closed off from the inmates. There's the smell of breath, funk, feet, the sound of music. On the bus, it was all that AND colors, the smells of perfume, the sounds of life. On the bus I could look out the window, with no bars in my way. I just sat back and put my MP3 player on, listened to music. I was in my own thoughts. I looked around in awe of everything I could take in.

We pulled into the bus station in Cleveland, Ohio, at 1:00 AM. The bus station was huge and FULL OF LIGHT. So much light. So much traffic, so many stores. So many people, all looking at their cell phones. It was strange. Now it's not like I came from another planet. I'm used to television, and I pretty much stayed abreast of the technology with newspapers, magazines and word of mouth from people coming in and out of prison through the years. It's one thing to read about it. It's totally different to witness it first-hand. I felt like FlyGuy when he got out of prison. "I'm gonna get you, sucka!" I had to be THE ONLY PERSON without a cell phone in the entire bus station.

Step 3 - A Couple More Stops - and Thoughts

We made a couple more stops on the route, just passed through some small towns. Soon we got into familiar territory, coming from the South Side of Chicago. I was singing to myself "Home Again" by Kanye West. The bus turned through the Chicago loop on Jefferson & Harrison at the Chicago Greyhound bus station. I remember vividly being in this bus terminal traveling from here to Iowa during my many drug transporting days. Not trying to glorify it. The past is the past. But seeing this bus terminal 16 years later AS A FREE MAN got to me.

I got off the bus for a brief layover, and went outside just to breathe. I could see that a lot had changed since I last spent some time here. There were quite a few additions to the place, changes for the better. But as I witnessed at the other bus stations, poverty was still present. Drugs and alcohol had had their affect on the bus terminal and the people who spent time there. The people who can't cope with life. Or should I say, the ones life had abused. Thinking about this sent me back down memory lane, thinking about how everything and everyone, including me, changes.

Step 4 - Destination - Cedar Rapids, Iowa

We were back on the road again, headed for my ultimate destination, Cedar Rapids, Iowa. Even though Chicago is the city that raised and made me the man I am today, Cedar Rapids, Iowa, is my second home. And I wanted to go back to the very town that I was convicted in. I wanted to go back with positivity, with a thirst for making things right. I got myself into that prison cell with all that time to serve. But I also believed with my whole heart that someone (or many people) could benefit from my story, could get some inspiration and motivation from my choices, my path, my outcome. I'm 100% sure that if I had been working a legit 9-5 job, 40 hours a week, there would have most certainly been a different ending to my story. But I didn't choose that path. I chose another. And I wanted to make something good out of it.

A whole day had passed with me stopping in different cities and changing buses. My arrival time was expected to be 1:00 PM. A quick stop in Iowa City, then the final leg of the journey to Cedar Rapids. During this time, I borrowed a lady's cell phone to make a few phone calls. My first call was to my favorite cousin Fe-Fe. She couldn't believe I was out! After that I called two partners of mine, the Big Homey Cortez and the OG Slim Houla Dula. It felt SO good to not hear an operator at the beginning of those calls! "This call is being monitored from a federal correctional facility." Not any more!

It was still feeling like a dream. I was 30 minutes away from seeing my mom, dad, brother, nephew and daughter. When I used to travel by bus from Iowa to Chicago and back, I would get so excited. This trip was no exception. One big difference, though, was that THIS time I wasn't high on drugs. Instead I was high on life. It was an amazing feeling. I was so excited to see my loved ones. And I was excited for them to see me as a free man.

On this final leg of the journey, my feelings were hitting me hard. I reminisced about the many family members and friends that were no longer with me in the physical form. Some passed before my incarceration. Like Johnell "Munchie" Harris. RIP Munchie. I said a silent prayer for Munchie. God have mercy on y'all soul. Time waits for no one.

Soon it was "Welcome to Iowa". I saw that a lot had changed just from where the bus was pulling up to. I could really see how the town had expanded. New buildings and businesses were everywhere. Just a reminder of how much time had passed.

Summation of the Journey

March 15, 2017 was one of the happiest days of my life. I knew things were only going to get better. The worst was behind me. I had my freedom, my family and a world of opportunity. All I wanted to do was keep living by the same set of rules in society that I lived by in prison. Those rules helped me get through my incarceration, and they would help me in my freedom.

The cab ride and the bus ride were all parts of my freedom ride, the ride to my freedom. The freedom ride was a chance to live it all again from a new position. A new outlook. The freedom ride was long, but it was an important rite of passage from the past, into the present, and even further into the future.

CHAPTER 4

Halfway is the Best Way

I spotted my darling mother, father, brother Myrail and my little nephew Robert outside of the bus station. It was one of the most beautiful sights I had ever seen. I embraced each of my family members. It was a feeling I can't really describe. I was truly blessed that after 16 long years it was FINALLY happening. I thanked God for allowing me this moment. I knew that things didn't have to go this way. Things could have ended so differently.

From the minute I got off the bus, my mom was recording my reentry into society from her phone. My brother went to his car and, like a true big brother, grabbed a gift he had for me - a Polo hoodie jogging suit with some Fresh Air Max and told me to throw that jail outfit and shoes into the nearest trash bin. I had already told myself that I wasn't going to be all into buying all the latest fashions. I wasn't going to spend my hard-earned money on clothes and material items that hold no real value. I was planning on shopping at the thrift store. But I had to appreciate and honor my brother, so I changed into the fresh jogging suit and shoes and put my prison outfit in the bags. The past, present and future all at the same time.

After all that it was time to get something to eat before making my way to the halfway house. The conversation in the car on the way to the restaurant was PRICELESS. It felt so good to be around family. In a car. With everyone healthy, drug-free and talking about God. Just wanting and having a better life. ALL POSITIVITY.

This was totally different from 16 years prior. See at that time, we were all getting high together. Doing all the wrong things. So now, on my reentry, I had to keep this in mind. You become the very people you're around. I knew I couldn't go back. They knew I couldn't go back. None of us could go back. It was a powerful feeling to know they had made the choice to move onto healthier, drug-free living, just like I was planning on doing. We all would be better together. My plan was this:

Keep God first in everything I do and say.

Don't mess with drugs, alcohol or anything that will alter my mind.

Stay as far away from negative people and toxic places as possible.

I did so much thinking while in prison, now it was time to execute my plan.

My first meal post-incarceration was at the Burger King that was en route to the halfway house. Burger King was so different than the chow hall! We were all so happy to be there together. I knew that meal was an answer to one of my mom's prayers. God's grace and mercy allowed this day to come. My daughter finally showed up and she greeted me with one of the tightest hugs, almost as tight as my nephew's, and HE hugged me for at least five minutes. The hugs from my daughter and my nephew were both full of so much energy. My daughter brought her boyfriend Jacob with her. I wasn't too enthused about that, but hey, she's not a little girl anymore, so I had to get up to speed with that whole situation. We ate, took pictures, and then it was time for me to get checked into the halfway house. My family went with me for that.

The Gerald R. Hinzman Center, aka the halfway house, is where I'd be setting up my new life. A halfway house is exactly what it sounds like; halfway out of prison, halfway into society. I've seen and heard from my time being locked up that some people are not successful in their first step, the halfway house. They can't even make it TO the halfway house. They let that fresh air hit them and whether it's friends, family, drugs or alcohol, they never make it to the halfway house or they're extremely late in arriving. I knew none of these scenarios was going to be the case for me. I wasn't going to jeopardize this new-found love for my freedom.

They say there's strength in being patient. When I tell you that I felt so strong about finally walking up those stairs into the halfway house after all this time, you need to know that's how I felt, and it was because I had learned patience. It was finally my turn after seeing so many brothers go in and out of halfway houses all over the country while I was locked up.

My mom and my brother had both been in the very same

halfway house, with the same halfway house workers and probation officers. Once we got inside, my mom and brother were greeted by people workers and officers who had been on this same journey with them. My mom had made it through the halfway house, and had made it through supervised release (I'll discuss that more later). My brother had made it through the halfway house and had only one month left of supervised release. Even with all those successes in my family, that was not a free ticket for me. I had to come into this with a good attitude and I had to do the right thing. They say you never get another shot to make a good first impression. I was ready to show the Hinzman Center staff the best version of myself, a mild-mannered, humble guy who was going to do the right thing every time.

First, I was introduced to Ms. Linda. She checked me in and asked me all kinds of questions. Next I was introduced to Mr. Scott. He searched my belongings and patted me down. This was different from routine searches I was so familiar with over the years. During those, you had to get fully undressed, lift your nut sack, squat, turn around, hold your butt cheeks and cough. I got so tired of that degrading process, but I got myself into that position, so I was willing to accept all that came with it. But that wasn't necessary at the halfway house. Another improvement.

While I was getting processed in, my mom and my brother had gone shopping to get me some sleepwear and personal hygiene items. When they got back with those things, Ms. Donna, a lady down the hall, talked a little bit to my mom. While that was going on, I saw a familiar face.

It was a guy called Black. I knew him from the first institution I was in, and I knew him pretty well. He wanted me to come into his room. So, I said my goodbyes to my mom and my brother, then headed in to visit with Black.

After visiting Black, I went to my own room. It was such a refreshing feeling. No sounds of keys jingling to unlock doors. A window you could actually open and shut! Most of all, not having to lay on that metal plate of a bed. There was a twin-sized bed in my room. Not my first choice, but I could tell that my dreams of laying in my own king-sized bed were getting closer and closer. This halfway house felt like a hotel to me. Not to mention it was co-ed, so females were there, as well. Females were one of the last things I was going to focus on. To me, they were a trap, something to be extra careful about. They were a test to see if I was going to be ready for society.

I slept so good the first night in the halfway house. The next morning, when I woke up, I couldn't believe that I was NOT incarcerated. I was still free. Even though it felt like I was still dreaming, this was my new reality. First thing, I met the morning staff, Mr. Pat, Ms. Chris and Ms. Courtney. I also got to see my probation officer Mr. Booty. Mr. Booty was a very nice, mind-mannered guy. Everybody had said to me, "You better hope you get Mr. Booty." It didn't really matter to me who I got. I was going to do the right thing and comply to all the rules that were laid down to me. Just the same, it was good to have a nice guy on my side.

Mr. Booty gave me the rules. He told me I was Federal Bureau of Prisons (FBOP) instead of Public Law. Public

Law was usually repeat offenders in the halfway house, and was limited to certain activities or destinations. For example, people in Public Law couldn't go to the YMCA. FBOP COULD go to the YMCA. You could have ONE shot to do the right thing. If you messed it up, though, you would go straight back to prison. It's severe. But I didn't have plans to test the waters. FBOP's rules were going to be fine for me.

My first breakfast, lunch and dinner were a whole lot better than the chow hall in prison. Meals here were more like a dining setting, and the food was like a five-star meal, a massive upgrade from the outdated, horrible food I ate for 16 years while incarcerated.

I knew a few of the guys in the halfway house. Some other guys had heard about me from guys traveling back and forth, in and out of institutions, guys who had been locked up with me in Pekin, IL, where I did the majority of my 16 years. The Federal system is so small and word of mouth travels fast. Especially word about your character. Everybody that has done time with me will agree that I'm a good dude with strong morals, and I always display integrity.

In the halfway house we had payphones. That was an improvement over the expensive calls you could make or receive in prison. At the halfway house we also had cell phones. We just could not bring them into the facility, we had to leave them in the hallway where there were mailbox shelves for your phone and charger. If you couldn't comply with these rules and got caught with your phone inside the halfway house, your phone got confiscated. Obviously, this was trouble that got attached to your name and reputation. Some guys just aren't going to follow the rules. But hey, my motto is if you can't follow these simple rules here, it's going to be really difficult once the box gets bigger and you're out of here. Look at it like this. The halfway house gives you enough rope to hang yourself. But why would you do that? I chose to ignore the rope.

In the halfway house we had a TV room, complete with different couches to sit and get comfortable. I didn't really watch TV, but I did sit down for a couple of movies here and there. Out the side door of the facility there was a smoking area. Guys could go outside to smoke for ten minutes, every hour on the hour. I'm not a smoker, but I would go outside just to look at the sky. The view was amazing. It was definitely worth the second-hand smoke I inhaled. I still couldn't believe I was there.

I spent those ten-minute intervals listening to guys talking about everything from the typical coming home from jail talk, messing around with girls talk, talking about getting high even though they knew that wasn't allowed. It was all in one ear, out the other. My main concern was DEON TERRELL HARRIS. I knew what I was about to do and, more important, what I wasn't about to do. I wanted my reentry to be a success, and I wasn't going to take any risks with my freedom.

You can get a pass to go out into society for several different reasons, to purchase hygiene items, go on personal visits, go to church. I got my first hygiene pass two days after I got into the halfway house. My two brothers Myron & Myrail, my mom and pop and I all went to the mall together. Lindale Mall had changed so much since I had last seen it. It was like walking into a carnival! The first thing that happened at the mall was that Myrail bought me an outfit, jeans and a t-shirt. That outfit cost $189! I knew I could've gotten a similar outfit from the thrift store and been just as happy with it. I didn't put value in the latest fashions. Like Vince Rames said in the movie "Baby Boy", "It's about guns and butter", and high price clothes are definitely butter. I wanted to return that outfit and get the money back, but it was a gift. Again I chose to honor my brother by accepting his gift graciously. Don't get me wrong, I'm not knocking anyone for wanting to wear expensive clothes, but just getting out of prison with hardly any money, expensive clothing isn't a very smart idea. I could see I was going to have to get used to accepting all gifts, whether from God or others, graciously.

My nephew Robert joined us later and gave me $200. Again I had to be gracious about this very subject! We all got a bite to eat, then headed back to the halfway house. Time was moving by so quickly, but I was moving right along with it. Per my goals, I arrived on time that time, and every time after that.

I experienced a lot in the halfway house that was integral to my successful reentry. One experience that was different than I thought it would be was housing after the halfway house. I had plans to stay with my mom after the halfway house, to save money. But they (the probation/supervised release officer) had other plans for me. I couldn't live with my mother because she was a felon that had been on supervised release before. So my mom moved next door to her apartment and I moved into her old apartment. Things couldn't have gone any better than that. It's so important to have that family support you, to have those family ties, while being back out in society. My mom was so helpful in so many ways that I can't even articulate. And I'm sure she doesn't know how helpful she was. I love her dearly and praise God every day he allowed her and my dad to be here with me on this journey.

Looking back on that situation, everything happened for a reason and turned out for the best. Sometimes what seems to be bad in the beginning is really a blessing in disguise. We must always remember that it's God's plan, "THY will be done" not "MY will be done". My time in the halfway house was a time of rebirth. I was like a child learning how to walk. The halfway house hosted reentry classes. They were facilitated by a lady named Judith. Judith was retired, but still took the time to share her wisdom with us, to help us be successful in our reentry. That was honorable and I appreciated that. She was a very wise woman. She handled tough subjects with humor. The class she taught touched on a lot of valuable things. One of those things was the importance of self-evaluation. We would sit around in a classroom and express different things about what was going on with us emotionally. She shared, too. (She shared how she loved Elvis Presley.) She cautioned us about sharing too much or sharing anything incriminating, because she would have to tell the authorities.

When you commit crimes, you separate yourself from society. You can't just walk back in and pick up where you left off. So part of reentry is getting reunited with society.

The Basic Essentials of Doing Time Constructively

For me, here's what that looked like.

I got a cell phone (that could be it's own chapter!).

I maintained my physical fitness by working out in the gym at the YMCA. Another kind of pass you can get at the halfway house is a walking pass. You earn this by complying with the rules. I used my walking pass to go jogging on the road outside of the Hinzman Center. I love running and clearing my mind. This is something I learned while incarcerated. Running was the only place where it was just me and God.

I had relationships with women. But I was scared of all of the different diseases that could be sexually transmitted. And I was also scared the guys that could be closely attached to women, from previous relationships. My first encounter with a woman was three months after I was out of prison. I made the conscious decision to engage with a woman who I had done some time with, so we were friends on some level. I didn't know if I was looking for a ride or die, but I had to start somewhere, and she was a good option. She picked me up from the halfway house (I had a hygiene pass). We went straight to the hotel right down the street. I was scared to death, thinking I was being trailed by staff from the Hinzman Center. The young lady told me, "Deon, calm down. Relax and enjoy yourself." That's what I finally did, and we had an amazing time. We hooked up a couple more times, then she moved out of town. We're still friends and talk from time to time.

I never complained, not one time, about anything while I was in the halfway house. I knew it was truly a blessing for me to be reunited with society and my freedom. All the guys that I had known that were still locked up, hoping to get out of captivity, made me appreciate my freedom even more. I made it through the halfway house with NO trouble because I wanted success and I knew that I was going to be successful. As part of my supervised release, I still go to the Hinzman Center to take my urinalysis. While I'm there, it's always a pleasure seeing the staff and the officers.

Being at the Hinzman Center was THE MOST important part of my reentry back to society. I was released on July 4, 2017, meaning I was there a little over four months. At that point I went to house arrest. I was still boxed in (no cage), but the box got a little bigger.

CHAPTER 5

This Game Is Economic

One of the most important resources you need in this world is money. You need it to buy food, water, clothing, shelter, entertainment. EVERYTHING. I knew before I was incarcerated how important it was. After my incarceration, I was painfully reminded of how important it was. I knew that in my successful reentry, my means to get money was going to be LEGIT and POSITIVE. I saw right off the bat how the value of a dollar wasn't much as opposed to 16 years ago. Back then a Big Mac meal was a little over $5. At reentry, in 2017, it was closer to $9. Daily living bills had to be paid, and debt I had accrued over 16 years ago (child support, driving fines, court fines) still needed to be paid. I was going to include those payments with my monthly bills. And I was going to do it all honestly and legally. I was going to have my wants and needs in check, and I was going to live within my means. I had to respect the DOLLAR. I needed to understand economics and use that understanding fully.

I knew a guy named Rio, aka "Goldie". He turned out to

be a vessel for me to write this chapter of this book. You see, he was the reason for my first job. He was working at a place called Precision Drywall and they were looking for laborers. He said you had to be moving all the time, and that it was hard work. He suggested I apply. Here is the rest of that story.

My first boss in my reentry was Dave at Precision Drywall. We met at the end of March 2017. I had been on home release for about two weeks. I had filled out the application a couple of days prior (on a recommendation from my friend Rio), then had an interview with the owner of the company. During the interview, we shook hands and introduced ourselves. He shared with me something simple but profound. He said, "Watch and keep control. Keep your eye on your pennies and the dollars will watch themselves." That made a lot of sense to me. Dave gave me a job, and an opportunity to be very smart in my finances.

After my interview with Dave, I met Ms. Christina Reel, the Controller at Precision Drywall. I still remember it like it was yesterday. Ms. Reel, a very nice woman, had me fill out some forms, handed me a hard hat, safety glasses and gloves, and told me to be ready to start the very next day. They were giving me a chance! They knew my background (fresh from prison) and were still willing to take a chance on me. I remember walking back to the Hinzman Center after that, feeling so good. That walk was one of the most peaceful walks of my whole life. That walk was a gift in itself. Breathing fresh air, being given a chance, and the confidence that I was going to keep being successful.

My first paycheck after my reentry was from Precision

Drywall. I worked HARD for that money. The check had MY NAME on it. At the halfway house, they keep 20% of your gross earnings. That bothered other people, but it didn't bother me. I looked at it like that was my rent, and I had to pay rent somewhere. Also, the Hinzman Center holds the majority of your money. They do that so when you go out into the world, you won't be completely broke. That's something not everyone understands. It's important to have a job PERIOD. And it's important to save money PERIOD. The Hinzman Center makes you do that. That's a blessing.

I made a list of goals I wanted completed. These goals were going to take precedence in my life. They were also going to take finances.

Goals:

Get my second book completed. I only had the manuscript typed from prison.
Pay all my fines.
Get my drivers license.
Get my own apartment.

By the grace and mercy from God, I completed all of those goals before I left the halfway house. I did all of this within 1 short year of working at Precision Drywall.

Money is important, but it's not the only thing of value. Time and experiences are also very valuable. Dave from Precision Drywall spent time with me, driving, sharing different life lessons with me. When the time came for me to move on to my next job, it was a hard decision to make. I weighed my options, and decided to take my excellent work ethic to the next company, Whirlpool. We all have to make decisions that are OUR BEST. There's only one you, and you are the ONLY one who knows what's best for you.

Remember, whoever ends up writing that paycheck with YOUR name on it, you need to be smart with your money. Trust the halfway house to help you develop good habits for your next phase of life. And pay attention to Dave's words. "Watch and keep control. Keep your eye on your pennies and the dollars will watch themselves."

CHAPTER 6

Self-Advocacy

As long as we're granted another day on God's green earth, we're all given one thing and that's twenty-four hours in a day. Now what you choose to do with it is left only up to you. You can choose to give up or give in. Whatever you're doing in life, whether it's good or bad, you can choose to give it your best shot. Or not. And that's what brings me to this chapter. Self-preservation, because at the end of the day, you are all you have, that person looking you dead in the eyes, no matter what, no matter where. You are the one person you can't get away from. So, my advice to you is to give that person the best of you that you can possibly give.

The one person on earth who knows what's best (or worst) for Deon Terrell Harris is Deon Terrell Harris. Not even my darling mother, who I love, adore and cherish, knows what's best or worst for me. And she gave birth to me! Now don't get me wrong, I listen to her advice and priceless wisdom, but I'm sure we've all heard the saying,

"What's good for you is maybe not good for me." It's kind of like this: We can both be physically sick, like having a cold, but the medicine is going to affect both of us differently. That's the uniqueness of us all. Like snowflakes, there's never one that is the same. So, we have to always put ourselves first, the main priority.

One of the things that keeps me focused on me is when I was in that courtroom and the Honorable Judge Linda Reade told me clear as day, "I sentence you to 360 months in the Federal Bureau of Prisons", then she pounded that gavel. That wasn't even two minutes, but my whole life changed and flashed before my eyes. And guess what? She sentenced ME. Only ME. No one else was going to do that time for me. Less than two minutes, and it was over. It was one of the best things that could have happened in my life. But to be clear, the point I'm trying to make is YOU are the ONLY PERSON in your life. So why not be the very best version of that person? We all have greatness inside of us. We just have to tap into it. You have to plan and structure your life and always believe in yourself. The only person besides YOU that you can depend on is GOD. No matter the situation, YOU always have the power to make the best decision for yourself. And when you don't feel like you have that power, turn to GOD.

CHAPTER 7

Faith - On God's Time

God is just waiting for you to begin to speak in faith. Every person has what they say. But besides words, you have to put the work in. It tells us that in the Bible. Faith without works is dead.

I'll use myself as an example. At this time in my life, I've been dreaming and envisioning myself doing things that I had NO idea how to do. I can dream because I have FAITH. My faith propels me. It moves me forward with God. But just because I'm ready, doesn't mean He's ready. We have to be prepared to move forward quickly. We have to always be in the faith, always be ready, so when God moves, we move. Just think about when I wrote my first book while in prison. I didn't know how it was going to get published. The first editor passed away while I was in prison! RIP Richard Matzke. But I kept the faith. I didn't give up in a place where dreams, aspiration, optimism and most of all faith are the exception rather than the rule. They are mostly unheard of. And now, by the same grace and mercy from God, I'm sitting in my living room writing my third book. A book that is reaching YOU. Had I chosen to not keep the faith, well...I'm not even going to give that thought any power! And neither should you. The best prayers and thoughts, the most satisfactory ones, are positive prayers and thoughts of faith.

If you think it and believe it, and every day you're doing something to go in that direction, you just might get it. It's simple. When God gives you an opportunity to think, visualize and change, you have to think, visualize and change. But before all that came FAITH. Remember, it all comes back to God. The Bible says, "What is done for man is not done completely by his faith, but by God through his faith."

And Michael Jackson (RIP) said it beautifully in "We're Almost There".

No matter how hard the times may seem,
don't give up your plans and dreams.
No broken bridge can turn us around,
cause what we're searching for will soon be found.

Keep the faith. When God moves, we move. Everything that needs to happen will happen. On God's time.

CHAPTER 8

The Formula

You have to find your own formula to make it in life. In this way, formula means pattern. I bet if you looked back on life, you'd see patterns. In my life, God is always on the mainline of all my movements and ideals. God is part of my formula. You need to find your own formula, and execute that formula, to make it in life.

I started thinking about this long before I came home from prison. See, while in prison, all you have time to do is think. So you think of plans, formulas. I thought so much in prison, I probably could have solved one of Einstein's numeric equations! Instead I solved an even harder problem: ME. I knew I had to submit to God, change my thinking, focus on the positive and set goals. That was so different from what I had done before my incarceration.

The phrase "If you keep doing what you're doing, you're going to keep getting what you got" kept popping up in my head. It's so true! So, I set some achievable goals. I start my day off listening to gospel music and meditating. I know that after that I'm going to work and punching a time clock. You best believe I'm putting myself in the right position before starting that day. My achievable goal is this: I'm putting myself and God first, so I'm going to start with music and meditation.

I don't "hang out" after work. Not trying to disrespect anyone, but I have a vision and God hasn't connected me to the right people to hang out with all the time. At this point, there's nothing out in the streets but trouble, jail, hospital or graveyard. My best friends are my mom, dad and brother. And they're the ones I spend most of my time with.

I don't mess with drugs or alcohol or any mind-altering substances. I must have a clear head at all times. Before my incarceration, my formula included drugs and alcohol. That was detrimental to my health and led to disaster. I'm not about to "keep doing what I was doing". I want different results.

There's nothing more important in one's life formula than freedom and peace of mind. I get these on a daily basis by following my simple formula. It works for me. I haven't been in a police car, I haven't been in jail, I haven't had to explain myself to a judge or probation officer. I hope and pray my formula is made up of the nutrients necessary for maintaining healthy growth. And if, like me, you've been on the other side of the fence, I hope you stay on the side where the grass is greener and filled with opportunity. It's so much better than the human warehouse where you're labeled and recognized by a number. When I was in prison, I had to put something new into my formula. That was writing. Guys in prison used to tell me, "Aw you're not about to write a book" and "You can't finish it". Guys, DOUBTERS, naysayers, would walk by my cell and try to observe me writing. I knew that I was not only giving myself an option once I was released, but that I could offer others a way out through writing. I ignored the doubt. I let them watch as reworked my formula for success and brought it to life before their eyes.

You have to focus on who you are. Put your lens on YOU no matter where you're at. I'm living proof that there's life after prison. But it's not going to be easy. Every day is a challenge and you have to constantly think of ways to get ahead and stay there. With positivity. You need to be smarter today than you were yesterday. Write your formula. Follow your formula.

CHAPTER 9

Grinding All My Life

In order for you to truly understand and know a person, you must first know some of the things he or she has been through, the good, the bad and the ugly. That whole thing is their story, and it shaped who they are. Let me tell you another part of my story, to help you understand me a little more.

Like Baby from Cash Money Records says, "If it's in you, it's in you". Even as a kid I was a hustler! Coming up on the West side of Chicago as a little boy I can remember going to the gas station to pump gas for little old ladies, helping those same types of ladies carry their groceries to their car, shoveling snow. I did what I had to do to make some money for candy. But some good can go along with that hustle. I was building communication skills, managing money, doing advertising and so much more at a young age. It wasn't til I got a little older that a negative force came into play, and that's when the drug selling started. After all that went down, the prison tactics used for survival kicked in. They became my new hustle. If it's in you, it's in you, right? I was a survivor and the hustle was part of that. But then, I was moved to create Progress Platform Productions. That became a new twist on an old hustle. It's always been in me. I just had to use it the right way. My books are one of the right ways to share my message.

I order my books wholesale so I can give them to people when I want to. Or I can sell them to people, sometimes face to face, sometimes through Amazon. I want people to know my story, all of it. One thing I do is I distribute my books in the same neighborhood that I used to hang out in, all day and night, selling and using drugs. Something guided me to drive to that same Sinclair station, park and set up shop right there. That was like my headquarters.

That part of town is referred to as the Lion's Den. It's the roughest part of Cedar Rapids, First Avenue by the Hy-Vee on the NE side of town. Sometimes I'd sell my books to people in Hy-Vee, sometimes the McDonalds right next door. I'd only sell there during the daylight. Darkness brings trouble. I once lived that life. I know how they think. Night time is the right time for all things chaotic and dangerous.

But during the daylight selling hours, I sold to people from all walks of life. I'd get so much love from everyone, including people who had been in the same type of struggle, and people who told me I was an inspiration and motivation. Thank God that a lot of people have never walked that path. But seeing that, and feeling that support, made me want to stay on the right path. They were motivated by me, but I was just as motivated by them.

I kept the books stashed in my trunk, then I sold them hand-to-hand. The author's notes in the back of the book tells you what's been prophesied. I'd walk around the parking lot in a circular pattern, passing Tasha's Beauty Shop, Unique Beauty Products, Stay Sharp, and Boost Mobile. I'd give my sales pitch and tell my story in the same spot that was used for negative reasons before. My story was written long ago. But the hustle changed for the better.

The first time I sold a book, that first legal transaction, was a rush. The currency exchanging hands, the honest appreciation of my work, the hope of making a difference. A RUSH! It was a similar feeling to selling narcotics, but there were some obvious differences.

I was going to be paying taxes.

I didn't have to worry about the police watching or taking me to jail.

The customers were feeling me

I love sharing my story, the story of my trials and tribulations. It's part of my new hustle. Praise God.

CHAPTER 10

Delegated Authority

The difference between a probation officer and a supervised release officer (SRO) is that the SRO is issued from the US Federal Bureau department. The SRO is your point of contact once you're out of the halfway house and off of house arrest.

I couldn't imagine what my SRO's preconceived ideas about me were. He knew I had done 16 years in federal prison. He knew I was a past substance abuser. He knew my mom and my brother Myrail, who were already part of the system and part of my criminal history. In fact, my SRO saw my brother while they were both at the federal courthouse seeing Myrail's parole officer for the last time. My SRO said to my brother, "I have your brother Deon." I couldn't help but wonder - what did this man think of me?

I understood that my SRO was a crucial part of my future success, the formula for my success. Besides me, he was the one who was holding the keys to my freedom. I wanted him to understand that I was a changed man. I wanted him to know I had respect for the law and authority. Lucky for me my SRO was a kind, understanding and fair person. I learned that he was actually rooting for me.

On one specific occasion, I had to be extra thankful for his positive position. My number got called to drop a urinalysis test. I got so busy selling and distributing my book that I actually forgot to go my drop. What are the odds that my SRO would show up at my book distribution "headquarters" at the very same time I was supposed to be dropping? Well, even though it wasn't likely to happen, IT DID. He saw me in action. He could see first-hand that I didn't miss my drop because I was doing something wrong. Instead he saw that I was doing something right. His grace got me a second chance. His grace showed me that I was on the right side of things.

One thing I've learned in life is that if you do the right thing, there's nothing but good consequences. I was in control of my freedom, just like I was in control of losing my freedom. My SRO could see that I was accepting and owning all of my actions, the good and the bad. He could see that I valued my freedom. Because of that, he allowed me some flexibility. One example of this was when I was working at Precision Drywall and had to travel to Iowa City every day. I wasn't supposed to leave town without calling first. My SRO waived that requirement for me so I could do my job without being hindered by that extra step.

That flexibility and grace opened many more doors for me. The "Living Beyond Prison Bars" foundation heard about me and my story. One of the founders of the foundation, Mr. Leon Kroemer, spoke to the other founder,

Ms. Sue Hutchins, and they personally invited me to speak to groups in Iowa City, Waterloo and Des Moines. It was such a privilege to speak to these groups of people in these different locations. I was also invited to speak at the halfway house's required drug class. It was truly an honor to be invited to these events and to be allowed to attend.

My SRO made house visits to my apartment and every time he found things to be completely intact. I know that he will never find something or someone that doesn't belong. I've been living a peaceful and serene life. My box is only going to get bigger, if I allow it to. Besides God and me, my SRO is the only gatekeeper to my freedom.

During a recent home visit from my SRO, I was asked about my next book. At that very moment, the Spirit led me to pick up a pen and share with the world the story of my reentry into society. My SRO always asks about sales of my previous books and whether or not he's going to be in my next book. Well, sir, you did more than make it into the book. You have your own chapter! Thank you for being an important part of my story. And thank you for giving me an opportunity to blossom.

CHAPTER 11

Obey or Pay

There's a saying that used to sound slick, but when you've observed it first-hand you know there's nothing slick about it. That saying is, "Crime pays". NO IT DOESN'T. It feels so good not running from the police - being able to drive next to, behind or in front of the police and knowing you're legit. See you have to obey the rules! Or you have to settle for the repercussions. Obey or pay.

During my incarceration, I saw so many guys I knew, some I had been very close to me, had lost their moms, dads or other family members. We're all going to leave this earth one day, but it really hurts when it happens and you can't say your final goodbyes because you're incarcerated. It's bad enough that you're hurting from not having your freedom. But that doesn't just hurt you. That hurts your loved ones, as well. It's not always a direct cost to you. Sometimes the cost is a missed opportunity to share in an important event. Obey or pay.

One thing about the streets is, they will implode on you.

If you don't understand the streets and without structure and obeying rules, your world will be like the wild, wild west. Why do you think there's so many killings in the world? First, it's a spiritual battle. Second, people on the street don't want to obey. I told myself while I was in prison that not only was I going to obey all rules, but I was going to be smarter and move smarter today than yesterday. One of the ways you can go about doing that is to choose to be motivated and not manipulated. Some people can be persuaded to do certain things they know they don't want to do and then they have to pay the price. The price is your FREEDOM. Obey or pay.

CHAPTER 12

Another Victory

One thing I've been stressing all through this book is that you're in control of yourself and your actions. When someone acts some type of way or says something to you that you felt wasn't right, the only thing you can control is how you respond. Life's not fair sometimes. No surprise there. If you ARE surprised, you're not getting it.

One thing is REAL and that's the choices we make. That's why for me, personally, I just set goals, took chances and discovered I can make it. I took everything God put in my life, good or bad, and learned from it. YOU CAN, TOO. There's nothing worse that a person can do to me that I didn't already feel when the judge told me I'd be serving 360 months. That was my low point. But I couldn't let that be the last word. I couldn't let that be how things ended up. That was not my legacy.

You have to get into position to put options in your life. Don't settle for just anything. This goes for jobs, relationships, ANYTHING. You deserve full happiness.

Racism still exists. It's just concealed. Maybe it's not even concealed so much anymore. But racism's been going on since the beginning of time and I don't think it's going to stop any time soon. This is the only time I'm going to refer to race. It's so important to stay out of prison, to stay productive, to work on things that are going to benefit you and your family, above all else. As a black man, it's even MORE important to stay on that path. We need to be setting good examples for everyone who's coming up after us.

It's ok to be driven by the green - we all know money is important. We all need that 9-5 to get established and to help meet our goals. I've been working since my release, and you should plan on that, too. Do your work and keep your eye on the prize.

At my trial, I was in front of an all-white jury. Not all white people are bad, some will help you. Same is true for blacks. Not all black people are bad. Some will harm you and some will help you. We need to always remember what Tupac said, "This is a white man's world". From being on the streets and being in prison, you, my friend, have seen things the average person hasn't seen. I thank God for discernment and for keeping me humble through it all. I know that the devil is trying me. He doesn't want to see me succeed. But God does. If the Lord Jesus Christ is with me, that's all I need. With that kind of crew, I'll remain victorious. And you will, too. It's nothing to be emotional about. It's just what works. Remember, don't get emotional, don't get even, don't get mad. Stay focused on your formula and you can start to depend on your responses. That's the road to victory.

CHAPTER 13

Figure It Out

My mom has many sayings that she shares with me, my siblings, my niece and nephew, anyone who she spends any time with. "Figure it out." Whenever she says that, my mind instantly goes to a maze or a very hard math problem. I should know better. She's talking about life.

There's only one you. No matter what life brings your way, you have to make the best decision. The decision that's going to put you into a better position. That's one of the most important things I want you to get from this book. No matter what life brings your way, you have to make the best decision. Sometimes you have to sit back and distance yourself from everything and everybody.

It so happened I was able to do that while I was incarcerated. I'm pretty much accustomed to sitting back all by myself, being still and getting instructions from God. There's a lot going on in this world and if you don't sit back and figure out what's most important to you, you'll be like a hamster on a wheel, going round and round, but going nowhere fast.

The clock doesn't stop for anyone. It won't stop for you, whether you have your stuff figured out or not. When it's your time to meet the creator, you're going to be in that casket, all alone. Yeah, people will come to your funeral, but it's just going to be you facing God. You owe it to yourself to think about and figure out how to get and stay ahead. And another word to the wise. YOU HAVE TO KEEP IT LEGIT AND LEGAL. I know that's easier said than done. But you have to put in the work. It's not just going to appear from out of the sky. Take it from me. You'll appreciate it so much more when you put in the legwork and when you start to see things prosper.

Don't let anyone tell you you can't do it! No one knows what's going through your mind. They haven't been through the things that shaped, molded and defined you. Once you figure out your plan, your formula, your goals, AND PUT GOD FIRST, you're well on your way to success. There aren't many people on this road. That doesn't mean they're bad or that they're not trying. It just means they haven't figured it out yet. But you, you reading this book, you got it. If you didn't have it figured out, you wouldn't have made it this far in the book. Praise God.

My road has been very long. It's been rocky at times, had a couple potholes and detours. But I know I'm on the right road. My journey has all been on God's divine calendar.

You're the star, the director, the captain of the ship called LIFE. There's no reset button. There's no stunt doubles. Make the best of it. I pray for all of us to win.

The Basic Essentials of Doing Time Constructively

Sometimes I think of life like it was a Rubik's cube. You keep turning it, moving it. You eventually figure it out. But I can't think of anyone who figured it out the first time they picked it up!

Sometimes I like to think of myself as a car. I was born in 1975, so I'm pretty much a classic. But everything wasn't properly maintained, so it needed some work.

I had to reconstruct all the wiring up under the hood - that's my brain.

I had to pull up into the shop and get some body work done - that was my physical being, needing to work out and to meditate.

I had to use good gas - cars run better with better gasoline. Using drugs and alcohol is the same as using poor quality gas.

Cars need tune-ups - so do humans. Go to the doctor regularly. Take care of things. Live by choice and not by chance. Things will run smoother.

CHAPTER 14

Passion Came From Pain

Being human means feeling pain at times. Being a reaction, pain can either bring out the best in you, or it can bring out the worst in you. For me, I want to limit the pain in my life. I don't want to feel pain. And I don't want to put my mom through any more pain. I strive to be the best me. I strive to find my purpose in life. God made us all with a purpose. With His help, we have to find our purpose. What I've learned is, even pain can help us determine our purpose. We don't need to avoid pain. Instead we should embrace it and where it has led us.

That doesn't mean you should go out of your way looking for pain. Think of life like a swimming pool. A swimming pool is a beautiful and dangerous thing, just like life. If your goal is to minimize pain, the smart way to do things is to start out in the shallow end until you have the skills to move into deeper water. Trying to go into the deep end before you have those skills is a sure way to feel pain. Instead of jumping into the deep end, unprepared and sure to create troubles, trials and tribulations, get in the shallow end. Use a mentor, use a life jacket, take some swimming lessons, make sure there's a lifeguard on duty. Learn from other people's mistakes and pain.

God is the lifeguard in the swimming pool of my life. And my swim coach is my mom. She's the best mentor for me. I hold onto to her every word. She speaks from experience in her own pool of life. Beyond that, she's invested in me, she has my best interest at heart. She wants to see me be able to use the whole pool safely and happily. Who is your mentor? Who has your best interest at heart? You need to find someone to fit that role. I can help if you need me. Reach out. Don't go into the pool alone.

You're going to make mistakes. That's why you need to have wisdom and understanding from God. He's your lifeguard. He's going to help you minimize your mistakes and live long enough to not make the same mistake twice.

When I speak on things God has delivered me from and that I've been through, I feel a burning in my gut. That burning is my purpose, my drive. I have a very strong desire to see God's prophecy for me fulfilled, to achieve my purpose. I'm not going to let God down. That burning is the feeling of sadness for my mother's prayers and tears. I won't let her feelings go in vain. That burning is the disappointment of my daughter growing up all those years without her daddy in her life. I won't let that go unchecked. That burning in my gut is my desire to pursue my purpose, passion and dreams.

I think about all I had to go through to get here. All of those things stoked the fire and desire inside of me and guess what? You possess the same fire and desire inside of you. It reminds me of the song lyric from the Wizard of Oz, "Oz never did give nothing to the Tin Man that he didn't already have." You have it. You just need to reach inside of you and grab it. Only the strong survive. You're strong.

When Judge Linda Reade gave me 360 months in her courtroom, I knew I had to share my story and to try to prevent anyone that came in contact with me from going through the pain of having their freedom taken away. And if it was too late for that, I knew I had to help those people get back on the right side of history. Helping others is part of my passion. I feed off of the positive feedback I get from people who've read either of my first two books. Every time someone feels moved to share with me, I say, "Praise God." Then I thank that person for being receptive to my pain, passion and purpose.

They say the best things in life are free. Pain can be one of the best things in life. Your pain is one of the main things that makes you YOU. It changed you. If all of your pain was gone, how would you identify YOU? Identify and embrace your pain and where it has led you. No matter where you're at at this moment, free or in a jail cell, you can make the best of your situation. Love yourself wherever you are. Feel your own pain, passion and purpose.

CHAPTER 15

Simply Beautiful

Writing this book has been a wonderful journey. Writing this whole series of books has been an even greater journey. I might not be completely where I want to be in life, but I'm a long way from where I was "once upon a time". Every day I do things that get me closer to my purpose. As long as I'm in the free world and maintaining, I'm successful.

My journey has been hard. I've gone through some extreme conditions. And I know I'll be going through more hard times. All of that is what gives my story more of an impact. Praise God for all that I've been through, the good and the bad. I mean that from the bottom of my heart, from the depth of my soul. My life has changed for the better. I want my story to have an impact on someone else's story, to help change their life. As long as I'm able to do that, I'm satisfied. I just love to see and hear that someone was moved and changed by my life. That's what it's all about - one person teaching another.

You can learn something from a child. You can learn something from a fool. You can learn something from someone who's walked a path like mine. Hopefully you've been moved by my words. I'm a productive member of society, a tax-paying citizen, a responsible black man. I get up and earn an income every day. That might not be a lot to some people. But to me it's EVERYTHING. I used to just be identified by a number, housed in that cell for 16 years. Now I'm a person, identified by a name. My name is on my lease, my paychecks, my bills. I own my car, and it has legit, proper license and insurance. I'm paying off my child support debt and all my other back bills. When I got out of prison, I had NO credit. Now my credit score is over 750. I've worked very, very hard to make my dreams a reality. And that was straight out of prison. If I can do it, YOU can do it. You just have to want it. You have to sacrifice for it. But you can DO it.

My motto is if it's not legal and from Uncle Sam, I don't want any part of it. In the circle of life the rules are pretty simple. But YOU have to be mindful of them, and you have to follow them. You have to surround yourself with the right people and eliminate the wrong people. Live a balanced life. Too much of anything is not good for you. In the bible it says "There's a time for everything". Once you are released, you'll be challenged with knowing the right time and place for everything - God, family, friends, substances, work, money, entertainment, relationships. You're going to have to keep a close focus on the right balance of mind, body and soul. And you CAN do it. Now that's simply beautiful.

ABOUT THE AUTHOR

Deon Harris is an up and coming urban literature author who aspires to be a substance abuse counselor and motivational speaker following his incarceration. Despite enduring the privations of prison life for over fourteen years, Harris is an extremely joyful and very grateful, individual who has an incredibly positive outlook on life.

This second title he hopes is beyond relatable and will inspire his readers to work towards the "blessed" life that he currently leads.

Order Form

MAKE CHECKS AND MONEY ORDERS PAYABLE TO:

Deon Harris
PO BOX 1025
Cedar Rapids, Iowa 52406

Name:_____

Address:_____

City:_____   State:_____
Zip:_____

Amount	Book Title or Pen Pal Number	Price
	Included for shipping for 1 book	$4 U.S. / $9 Inter

This book can also be purchased on:
AMAZON.COM/ BARNES&NOBLE.COM

We Help You Self-Publish Your Book
**You're The Publisher And We're Your Legs.
We Offer Editing For An Extra Fee, and Highly
Suggest It, If Waved, We Print What You Submit!**

Crystell Publications is not your publisher, but we will help you self-publish your own novel.

Don't have all your money? …. No Problem!
Ask About our Payment Plans
Crystal Perkins-Stell, MHR
Essence Magazine Bestseller
We Give You Books!
PO BOX 8044 / Edmond – OK 73083
www.crystalstell.com
(405) 414-3991

Plan 1-A 190 - 250 pgs $719.00   Plan 1-B 150 -180 pgs $674.00
Plan 1-C 70 - 145pgs $625.00

2 (Publisher/Printer) Proofs, Correspondence, 3 books, Manuscript Scan and Conversion, Typeset, Masters, Custom Cover, ISBN, Promo in Mink, 2 issues of Mink Magazine, Consultation, POD uploads. 1 Week of E-blast to a reading population of over 5000 readers, book clubs, and bookstores, The Authors Guide to Understanding The POD, and writing Tips, and a review snippet along with a professional query letter will be sent to our top 4 distributors in an attempt to have your book shelved in their bookstores or distributed to potential book vendors. After the query is sent, if interested in your book, distributors will contact you or your outside rep to discuss shipment of books, and fees.

Plan 2-A 190 - 250 pgs $645.00   Plan 2-B 150 -180 pgs $600.00
Plan 2-C 70 - 145pgs $550.00

1 Printer Proof, Correspondence, 3 books, Manuscript Scan and Conversion, Typeset, Masters, Custom Cover, ISBN, Promo in Mink, 1 issue of Mink Magazine, Consultation, POD upload.

We're Changing The Game.
No more paying Vanity Presses $8 to $10 per book!

Made in the USA
Monee, IL
10 July 2024